Hagar Figler

Does Terrorism have a Gender? - The Place of Women in Global Islamic Terrorism

GRIN Verlag

Bibliografische Information der Deutschen Nationalbibliothek:

Die Deutsche Bibliothek verzeichnet diese Publikation in der Deutschen National-
bibliografie; detaillierte bibliografische Daten sind im Internet über http://dnb.d-
nb.de/ abrufbar.

Imprint:

Copyright © 2008 GRIN Verlag GmbH
Druck und Bindung: Books on Demand GmbH, Norderstedt Germany
ISBN: 978-3-640-14354-2

This book at GRIN:

http://www.grin.com/en/e-book/114041/does-terrorism-have-a-gender-the-place-
of-women-in-global-islamic-terrorism

GRIN - Your knowledge has value

Der GRIN Verlag publiziert seit 1998 wissenschaftliche Arbeiten von Studenten, Hochschullehrern und anderen Akademikern als eBook und gedrucktes Buch. Die Verlagswebsite www.grin.com ist die ideale Plattform zur Veröffentlichung von Hausarbeiten, Abschlussarbeiten, wissenschaftlichen Aufsätzen, Dissertationen und Fachbüchern.

Visit us on the internet:

http://www.grin.com/

http://www.facebook.com/grincom

http://www.twitter.com/grin_com

The Place of Women in Global Islamic Terrorism:

Does Terrorism have a Gender?

Seminar: Gender and Terrorism

Lauder School of Government and Diplomacy

Interdisciplinary Center Herzliya

Semester 2008

By: Hagar Figler

Index:

Introduction:

In the western world, the participation of women in higher ranked positions is no longer questioned. The equality between man and woman is considered a given fact. However, in regards to terrorism, the difference in gender is still considered an issue, and femininity and masculinity plays a role. The gender theory, the significance of being a man or a woman, has gone into new dimensions, by affecting fundamental Islam and giving terrorism a new identity. Years ago, the occurrence of suicide bombings was considered the embodiment of "evil", and had evoked from the public consternation and incomprehension. Today, these one-time occurrences have become a recurrent trend, known as a martyr phenomenon, heard daily on news. Up until recently, most of the suicide bombers, known as "Shahids", were men who committed the act in order to be remembered in history and upon being promised that it will lead them to paradise. However today we see more and more women, especially Muslim/Islamic women, who decide to die as "female martyrs".

Since the attack on the World Trade Center in September 11, 2001, terrorism has become a matter of every-day public issue, discussed as one of the top topics in daily news. However, these discussions rarely focus on the implication of gender on the issue, and Islamic terrorism is intuitively perceived as "masculine" rather than "feminine". When the issue of gender in the Islamic world is finally brought up, the focus is usually around the political and domestic oppression of woman, an issue that has been analyzed thoroughly by political scientists, legal practitioners and historians from all perspectives. However, rarely is the feminine role, or lack thereof, discussed in the pretext of terrorism. No public emphasis has been given to the question, of how is it possible that these all-around oppressed women, whose role in their society, by stereotype, is to be the caring housekeeper - to give birth to children, to stand for values like education, etc. - have suddenly taken the role that has long been reserved for men, by turning to violence and volunteering for suicide missions.

It begs the question, does terrorism have a gender? Is terrorism a "masculine" means, increasingly utilized by Islamic women to raise their low standing in society and achieve liberation? Is it used by women because "only with the weapon of the classical symbol of masculinity and with particular cruelty, [an Islamic female may achieve] the conception to be a perfectly emancipated woman[1]"? Or, is terrorism merely a "unisex" act of war that so happens to be used by women? When a woman takes on a suicide mission, is she doing it as an Islamist fundamentalist, in the name of Islamic liberation, or is she doing it as an oppressed feminist, in the name of women's emancipation? Some would claim that neither answer is correct, that no political or social significance should be attributed to women's involvement in terrorism, because Islamic women are incapable of taking a stance, and therefore any involvement they may have is individual, due to personal agony, rather than collective, in the name of higher aims.

This paper will reflect on the phenomenon of Islamic female suicide bombers, using fundamental palestinian women and their individual case patterns, to analyze the impact of gender issues in the context of Islamic terrorism. The case patterns will show empirically that females who took part in terrorist activities, unlike most of their male counterparts, were not purely driven by Islamic liberation motivations, and took into consideration additional factors, such as personal circumstances that left them with nothing to lose or a thirst for revenge. Though no case has shown that a palestinian woman was motivated in the name of female emancipation alone, it will be argued that the byproduct of the phenomenon, perhaps subconsciously, is the beginning of feminism in the Islamic world.

Gender Distinctions: Women and Terrorism

Gender:

While "male" and "female" are sex categories, "masculine" and "feminine" are gender categories. According to the World Health Organization, "gender" refers to the socially constructed roles, behaviors, activities, and attributes that a given society considers appropriate for men and women[2]. And so, while aspects of sex do not vary substantially between different human societies, aspects of gender vary greatly.

---

[1] "Der Spiegel" (German: "The Mirror"), 1985.
[2] http://www.who.int/topics/gender/en/

4

Feminism:

Feminism focuses with gender inequality and places an emphasis on women's rights, with an active desire to change the status of women in society. Furthermore, feminists emphasize the relationship between the genders as a primary vehicle for the oppression of women[3].

Defining the Gender association:

Radical female "aggression" is rather masochistic in its nature and women tend destroy themselves, instead of destroying others, like it is oftentimes the case with extremist men. Sadistic women are an exception. In this connotation, one tends to search for reasons; in what family environment she has been raised and to what extend she got socialized. In fact, it seems "unnatural" that women are capable of violence and as a suicide bomber one may actually don't want her to be able to help what she has done. Most preferably one lays the blame on the cruel father, husband, brother or other male relatives, who coerced her in the first place. However, fact is, that women not only destroy themselves, but also other by committing a suicide attack. It is a myth to assume that women are pacific and these female committers are an exception of the rule. They have always existed, such as the women who guarded in the concentration camps during the Nazi regime. If one assumes, that Islamic women are victims, their status of being or being treated as an object ceases. The idea, that a woman acts inhuman out of her own accord, may nevertheless seem to some of us absurd. A female suicide bomber proofs the opposite and breaks therewith a taboo on two levels. She not only violates against the norm of the civilized Human being, she rather than goes actually one step further and joggles the foundations of the idealized image of women within Islam. All of the sudden the biological gender plays a role. Yet, the question remains if there is "female sadism".

Between the cruelty of women and men there is not necessarily a difference, since both genders have most likely been taught sadism during their childhood, by both their parents and educator. They most likely have been treated with cruelty or even in a perverse manner and were not allowed or couldn't to defend themselves, according to the Swiss psychoanalyst Alice Miller.[4] The coil of torture and being tortured sustains within men and women.

---

[3] http://plato.stanford.edu/entries/feminism-topics/
[4] http://www.datum.at/1005/stories/1113078/

However, it is usually the parent's responsibility and subsequently the society who transmit the aggressions to the children.

Gender roles within Islam:

Many Muslims "scholars" and western feminists are quite passionate in discussing the status of Muslim women within Islam. However, while there seems to be a common theme to these discussions, they do not address the core issues surrounding gender roles in the same manner. Both, feminism and Islam have their own recognition of women's rights. They differ, however, in how they attempt to realize these rights. Feminism favors changing social perception of women using law while Islam favors molding social perception of women to fit the ethical regulations of Islam and the Quran[5]. This difference in mentality creates a conflict, whereby feminism, which views the engagement between men and women as liberating[6], clashes with the Islamic understanding that the isolation of women contributes to her personal and to her family's honor.

Feminism favors understanding and then redefining gender roles and relations in a given society. Islam, on the other hand, has rigid gender role definitions, which are not open for redefining, since they are viewed as inflexible, being derived from the biological sex. In Islamic societies, taking care of children and the domestic sphere in general, is understood to be one of the most important, if not the only, responsibility of a woman. That is not to say that a Muslim woman cannot join the paid labor force. However, the status of motherhood is so highly-ranked in Islamic societies, that it presents a challenge to the idea, that gender roles are socially created rather than biologically given.

The role of men and women within Islamic societies and terror organizations:

Gender differences can also be seen among male and female terrorist. The demand for male terrorists is much higher than it is for female terrorists, as organizations are much less open to recruiting females to their force. This means that a male terrorist has a variety of organizations to choose from, whereas a female terrorist might become active in an organization which does not fully represent her views and ideals, simply because no other

---

2 http://www.pickledpolitics.com/archives/999

organization is willing to recruit her due to her gender. Furthermore, while there are many training camps for male terrorists, there is only one known training camp for female terrorists (sponsored by the Al Aqsa Birgades female terrorist organization named after Wafa Idris), which means women who decide to engage in terrorist activities are far less trained and experienced.

Another aspect that is different between the genders is their way of dealing with emotions. While women tend to disconnect themselves in times of distress[7], men are more prone to act out on their feelings and are therefore considered more emotionally reliable in completing suicide missions. AlAqsa Martyrs Brigade in Jenin leaderm Zacharia Zubeidi, claims that the "emotions of girls are higher then boys. Their feelings are much deeper than boys. God created girls more sensitive... we decided no girls.... A girl has few choices. She cannot go and shoot. Every girl has just one way-a (bombing) operation[8]."

The recognition given to each gender in respect to their terrorist activities is different as well. Contrary to men, women who choose to become suicide bombers are viewed as martyrs and reach a star-like status only after death, upon a successful mission. It should be noted that this status is not reached, and the woman does not receive that same recognition if she fails in her attempt.

Overlook into history:

The best known historical ancestors of the suicide attackers of today are "the assassins" from the 11th century, also known as a sect of Shiite Muslims who used assassination as a tool for purifying the Muslim religion.[9] Legendary are their excessive feasts and also their assassinations in which they risked their own lives. They valued their own death as "martyrdom for the glory of god". The "assassins" however, were target-oriented in their killings, seeking to assassin high-ranked individuals, unlike today's "martyrs", who randomly and coincidently murder people.

In terms of female involvement, there several examples of female "martyrs" in Islamic history. The most prominently-known woman is probably Nusayaba bint K'ab, who,

---

[7] Speckhard, Anne. "Understanding Suicide Terrorism: Countering Human Bombs and Their Senders" in Topics in Terrorism: Toward a Transatlantic Consensus on the Nature of the Threat" (Volume I) Eds. Jason S. Purcell & Joshua D. Weintraub Atlantic Council Publication 2005, page 16

[8] Speckhard, Anne. "Understanding Suicide Terrorism: Countering Human Bombs and Their Senders" in Topics in Terrorism: Toward a Transatlantic Consensus on the Nature of the Threat" (Volume I) Eds. Jason S. Purcell & Joshua D. Weintraub Atlantic Council Publication 2005, page 17

[9] http://lexicorient.com/e.o/assassins.htm

according to the legend, fought alongside her husband and two sons in the caliphate of Abu Bakr, and suffered eleven wounds and an arm loss. It has been told that several female relatives of the prophet Mohammad, such as his wife Aisha or his granddaughter Zaynab bint Ali, have also been active in the Jihad.[10]

However, these historical figures have barely been used as role models. Instead, examples from more recent history are usually used, such as Loula Abboud or Wafa Idris. Loula Abboud was the first women in the Middle East to blow herself up, in April 1985, after Israeli soldiers had taken actions against her guerilla group. Her story was notable because she was a Christian and communist, and therefore did not fall into the usual profile of an Islamic bomber. Wafa Idris became a Palestinian hero and role model in 2002, as the first Palestinian woman to carry out a suicide attack in Israel. An Egyptian newspaper even went as far as to call her "the bride of heaven, who preferred death over the amusements of life" and a "powerful message for the Arabic nation".[11]

Facts and Arguments:

It is taught in Islamic societies, that carrying out a suicide mission leads to heaven, where everyone is equal. However, it seems as though in this world, even in death, women are not treated equally when it comes to the compensation paid by Hamas, Islamic Jihad or the Palestinian National Authority for carrying out suicide missions. According to analyst Barbara Victor, whereas families of male suicide bombers receive a lifetime pension of about $400 per month, families of female suicide bomber rarely receive half of that amount[12]. Furthermore, as stated above, it is evident that female terrorists do not receive the same star-like treatment upon their death as their male counterparts.

---

[10] http://lexicorient.com/e.o/assassins.htm
[11] Middle East Media Research Institute (MEMRI) Internet Site, "Wafa Idris: The Celebration of the First Female Palestinian Suicide Bomber- Part I,II,III)", February, 2002 (www.memri.org)
[12] Barbara Victor, Army of Roses: Inside the World of Palestinian Women Suicide Bombers. Rodale, 2003.

Woman within terrorist organizations

Which role do women play in Islamic terror organizations? Does an image of a women exist, upon which behind every strong male terrorist stands a female terrorist or is the Islamic women narrowed on "children, kitchen and Mosque"? Answers to this question, why women actually become terrorists, are usually biased. It is presumed that the "soft and weak" gender mainly joins the militant Jihad because of emotional and social reasons such as family attachment, death of the husband or just naivety. Marc Sageman, who analyzed in his survey "Understanding Terrorist Networks" the social connections of these women and yet he came to a totally different result. Women are significant actors within the terror networks and oftentimes even more radical than men.[13] Indeed there are cases, were raped Muslim women join terror organizations because, in the view of their family and society, they are dishonored and therefore not marriageable. Failed Shahidas from the Palestinian territories have given these as their rationale. But why would they, in the attempt of ending their own lives, also want to end other people's life at the same time? Here comes the incentive system of the Islamists into play, from the promised spot in paradise to the there waiting man of her dreams up to the financial coverage of the family through the terror organization, commissioned by them. Furthermore do political and ideological motives play a vast role, such as the war against the occupying power or believe in the superiority of Islam. Osama Bin Laden had 1996 clearly expressed in his famous fatwa "the declaration of war against the USA and the west "and furthermore, that women play a significant role in the Jihad: "Our women…motivate and comfort their sons, brothers and husbands to fight against the enemy."[14] Interestingly has the role and exposure of the women in his following fatwa, 1998 "Jihad against Jews and crusaders" been left over. In the Palestinian Hamas this development proceeded on the contrary. Initially the leader of the Hamas, Sheik Yassin, had refused to implement women as suicide bombers. The success of this strategy in the Lebanese Hisbollah, Al-Aqsa-Brigades and the "Palestinian Islamic Jihad" persuaded him, to use women as a "reserve army" which can be used if required, which was furthermore implemented. Suicide attacks are anyhow a cost-efficient, technologically easy and with a loss risk affiliated weapon. Hence, women can be best assured; they seem less suspicious and are being less strict controlled by security forces. They become cheep weapons in the hand of male terrorists. Next to this tactical advantage, there are enormous strategic advantages, since attacks made by women attract a vast media interest. Hence, the aims of spreading fear and

---

[13] http://nlarchiv.israel.de/2003_html/05/220503a.htm
[14] http://nlarchiv.israel.de/2003_html/05/220503a.htm

horror and the indication of political ambitions are therefore best achieved. Women serve rather as sympathy bearer; the media is more interested in their motivation, personal and family situation. As a side effect, the recruitment of women as suicide bombers also increases the recruitment of men who volunteer out of shame. Female suicide bombers have many advantages for the male terrorists and the women also pledge something out of it, to die for Islam.

According to Sheikh Yussef al-Qaradawi, female suicide bombers are "heroes of our time who sacrifice themselves as a living bomb for Islam."15 The fact that Sheikh Yussef al-Qaradawi supports the Palestinian suicide commando is since 1995 clear. Already at that time he released a fatwa which indicates the suicide attacks in Israel as accurate Islamic. His female fans appreciate him mainly because he sticks up for the "emancipation" of the women. In the same degree he praises the female suicide bombers. Women who are less brave, however who are ready for combat, he suggests "the economic Jihad", hence the holy war of boycotts, such as the prevention of buying Coca Cola, McDonald's and Pampers, hence western products.[16]

The well known Wafa Idris case has broken the myth of pacific women. Even if these women are taking in most cases the victimhood, in the perception of the public they become either monsters or icons. Wafa Idris for instance became a monster. Up to now, women in the Palestinian occupied territories had been used as cannon fodder. In the hierarchic structures of the terror organizations they have never truly been integrated. However, this has recently changed. Samir Sabih takes over a pioneering role as the first female bomb constructor in the history of the conflict. Sabih had been send by the radical Islamic Hamas to the West Bank in order to train new explosive experts. Therewith she is no longer a ticking time bomb rather than an acting manipulator. "This is an unusual turn. This would rather fit into the spectrum of an emancipated idea, that women take part in the battle. And this I regard as by far much more frightful," said Dr. Deborah Heifetz-Yahav, the Israeli anthropologist and staffer at the International Policy Institute for Counter-Terrorism in Herzliya, Israel.[17] Indeed there have been female terrorists in the past, as the most famous example of modern international terrorism in the Middle East is, up until now Leila Khaled, who in the seventies on behalf of the Palestinian liberation front PFLP had been involved in the plane highjack. As a result she had been made the "Pinup girl of Terrorism" by the boulevard, inspiring hundreds of other young women around the world who admired her thrilling and famous pictures in the

---

[15] http://www.zeit.de/2002/37/Globalisierung_auf_Islamisch
[16] http://nlarchiv.israel.de/2003_html/05/220503a.htm
[17] http://www.datum.at/1005/stories/1113078

media.[18] The killing part she had normally left to the men. The cliché of the sacrificing mother, who is not capable of taking someone's life, has been at the latest with the attack of the mother of two children, Reem Reyashi, once and for all disused. Regardless if mother or not, women are capable of anything.

In contemporary terrorist spheres one knows by now how to use the cliché of the "weak gender". Female, innocent and highly explosive, this becomes a surety for a media efficient performance. From day to day it is managed to higher the attention of the media, through women. Still, the terrorists know by now how to capitalize on women and train them to become female suicide bombers, though recruitment or even through force by their "Muslim brothers". Only every tenth woman acts on behalf of revenge, they aren't brave avengers rather than desperate women who are seeking for acknowledgment. In the Palestinian society, Shahida's enjoy a hero status likewise their male combatant. According to Dr. Deborah Heifetz-Yahav:" Ever since a woman blew herself up, this challenged the Hamas to consider woman in the participation of terrorist activities, which can be regarded as an emancipating act".[19] In fact, the Hamas and the Islamic Jihad had in the beginning of the first intifada pointed out, that they won't allow the recruitment of women. At the same time had the, in the meantime passed away, head of the PLO, Yassir Arafat appealed for "equality": "Women and man are equal. You are my army of the roses, which will destroy the Israeli tanks!" [20]In the afternoon of January 27th 2002, the same day he made this announcement, the first Palestinian woman, Wafa Idris, blew herself up in a shopping mall in Jerusalem. One suicide attack and one month later, the in the meantime murdered Sheikh Ahmed Yassin, the spiritual leader of the Hamas, enacted a fatwa which admitted women the right to aggrandize themselves to paradise though suicide attack. I beg to believe, that this can be considered as an act of emancipation, rather than a perverse understanding of equality. Furthermore, many women choose violence for political or religious reasons just as men do, however it is hard to believe that they do it for emancipation reasons or aims. The issue of the rights of committing an attack by women wasn't accumulated by women, but rather by men, who consider female suicide attacks as heroic. According to Natasha Khalidi, who is a Palestinian women activist, in one way or another, "women set a statement", which is the participation within the national resistance.[21] The Wafa Idris case proofs, that it less concerned a political act, rather than an

---

[18] www.fas.orf/irp/threat/frd.html, page 49
[19] http://www.datum.at/1005/stories/1113078
[20] Barbara Victor, Army of Roses: Inside the World of Palestinian Women Suicide Bombers. Rodale, 2003.

[21] Catharine Goldsmith, "Terrorists because They are Women" (Intersec, 1992) pp.26

attempt of evasion of a marginalized woman who got divorced because she couldn't give birth.[22] The 27 year old Idris was not randomly chosen. Idris was a divorcee who couldn't give birth throughout her nine years of marriage. Furthermore she suffered under the bad relationship she had with her older brother, who since the death of the father became the dominating man in her life. Since then, she was ready for any sort of escape. In the traditional Palestinian society a divorced and childless women becomes a burden. Women like Idris don't get the chance to get remarried. For the responsible members of the Fatah are women like Idris, who don't comply the social norms, easy pickings. Female suicide bombers have many advantages for the male terrorists and the women also pledge something out of it, to die for Islam. Rim Raishi is the first Palestinian women from the Gaza strip, who sacrificed herself as a "living bomb" in the fight against the State of Israel. [23]

Terror organizations and their impacts on women

For the Al-Qaida the recruitment of women in „the war against the crusaders ", it is rather a deviation of their patriarchic fundamental law. Women should stay at home and take care of the children. War is a pure male business. Palestinian female suicide bombers volunteer for such operations and, most of the time, they are not even trained nor did they get mentally prepared for the mission. There are two rationales for that, to begin with, because they are not welcomed into the by male dominated divisions and secondly, the psychological brainwash of propaganda against Israel had always been an element in their lives. With this opinion the Al-Qaida didn't for too long stand alone. In the Al-Qaida occurred a change of policy officially in August 2004 with the internet magazine "Al Khansa" (Holy female warrior). The female editors, a "women information desk of the Arabian Peninsula", demanded there to "support our men in the

battle". [24]Jihad is a personal duty, where the woman is equal to man, furthermore she doesn't need to ask for permission from anyone, neither from the parents nor husband. This is, in a male dominated society, an extraordinary type of "emancipation" in order to reach and get the right to blow yourself up when and were ever a woman wants. Since they could strike anywhere and anytime, they spread fear and horror. At the same time they label their own group as a defenseless victim of an overpowering aggressor. It seems as if the desperation is

---

[22] Middle East Media Research Institute (MEMRI) Internet Site, "Wafa Idris: The Celebration of the First Female Palestinian Suicide Bomber- Part I,II,III)", February, 2002 (www.memri.org)

[23] http://www.datum.at/1005/stories/1113078

[24] http://www.heise.de/tp/r4/artikel/21/21815/1.html

enormous, so that there is the "must" to blow oneself up in order to escape reality. This effect is even more intensified by women.

Influence of the media

An essential calculus behind the female "martyr operations" is the media effectiveness. The interest in the medial realization of suicide attacks is large. The business with the "unimaginable" and the "horror" runs good, above all with female suicide bombers, especially in the west. Normally one doesn't expect from a woman such "inhuman" action. There it becomes a matter of the clichés, of the female gentleness or the caring role of the mother. One looks at the women rather as victims of violence, rather than victimizers who carry out violence. This perception creates the "tremendousness" and the "stupefying", which is aimed against any humanness. If the female attacker is pregnant, which was a few times the case, or she leaves behind children and husband, this represents one higher step on the psychological ladder of the incomprehension and of the horror. For the initiators of the attacks is the media very useful. The news coverage calls attention for the grievances which they suffer under, as well as on the goals which they fight for and it is at the same time an advertisement for new recruits. Thus there is no wonder, that almost 40% of all Muslim "Martyrs" are in the meantime women.[25]

Palestinian female suicide bombers: New social and religious motives

The issue, why Palestinian women hire themselves as suicide bombers has raked many people's brains. Symposia and conferences were held and many academic and journalistic articles have been written about this phenomenon. Wafa Idris, the first Palestinian suicide bomber in Israel, consistently serves as a figure as well as an example for the repressed women in the Islamic male society. She murdered in order to regain her once lost honor in the Islamic society. Wafa could not give birth and her husband therefore divorced her. As a worthless woman, who stands outside the society, she had rescued her honor as well as her families honor by choosing the "martyr death". It seems like an easy prey for the indoctrination through terrorists. It's noticeable, that the women are being entrapped to the evil action which they truly don't seek; however the social circumstances drift these women

---

[25] Barbara Victor, Army of Roses: Inside the World of Palestinian Women Suicide Bombers. Rodale, 2003.

into deadly fatalism. It is not compulsory as a woman to die for an ideology, political and religious aims. It is important to mention, that most Shahidas originated from a more secular background. [26]

Regarding the cause of this phenomenon, it has been hardly spoken about. In fact, is there is no comprehensive profile of female suicide bombers. The motivations, concomitants and personal stories are too diverse. The Iraqi woman and her husband aimed to blow themselves up in the SAS Radisson Hotel in Amman and did this apparently out of revenge for her by the US army killed brothers. Many Chechen women take revenge for the mass rapes through Russian soldiers. For women of the Tamil tigers had sexual abuse and torture played an immense role. In Palestine a "martyr" becomes a hero, whose picture is handing all over house walls, a sigh of deathlessness. The social reputation of the family rises, in some cases they even receive some money, which pays for the education of the siblings.[27] There is also another motivation, such as the unbearable life under the Israeli occupation, the ongoing discrimination and humiliation of Israeli soldiers, being locked behind walls and the restriction of weather to choose to drive somewhere one wants, basically like in prison. In this situation death in paradise and the eternal life might seem attractive to these women. It certainly can be seen as a "pseudo" act and type of emancipation, however not as the western emancipated women has known. For the first time, Islamic women perform by themselves without asking for permission from anyone. Not only men are proud worriers, women also, all of the sudden, "equalized" in the male dominated domain, moreover, women are martyrs for themselves and their own folk. This proofs, that the religious aspect of committing a suicide attack is not necessarily the main argument, especially in the case of a woman attacker. Religious aspects however, can not be avoided regarding Shaidas and their motivations, since they are deeply rooted within their social religious life, which can be one way of escaping it. If a woman decides to become a Shahida, it proves the fact that she has already ended to live her and this life.

Terror organizations recruit besides men and children also women as suicide bombers. Just as children, women arouse less suspicion. Furthermore, their checking seems to be by far more problematic, a man may just pull up his shirt in order to prove that he doesn't wear an explosive belt. Regarding to women, such security procedures aren't that easy to perform.

---

[26] http://www.heise.de/tp/r4/artikel/21/21815/1.html
[27] http://www.heise.de/tp/r4/artikel/21/21815/1.html

Women as suicide bombers aren't a definite novelty. Already in 1985, seventeen year old Lebanese named Sana Mehaydali, detonated herself by order of the pro-Syrian terror group near an Israeli military patrol.[28] However, a new phenomenon has accrued in the past years, where women are being recruited through Islamic organizations like the Islamic Jihad and the Hamas, altough they fundamentally contradict the social-traditional and religious norms. Given that the preparations for a terrorist act requires several activities, where women stand in close contact with men, whom they neither are related nor married to. Women are mostly being recruited for civil target operations, like the 29 year old Hanadi Jaradat, who detonated herself in October 2003 in the Maxim Restaurant in Haifa, where 19 people lost their lives.[29] During the period of recruitment of women, the Islamic Jihad and the Hamas reflect the personal circumstances of the candidates and present thereby oftentimes the martyr death as the most advantageous solution in case of a private conflict situation, such as divorce, unfaithfulness in a marriage, illegitimate sexual intercourse etc. Sheik Ahmed Yassin explained the purpose of legitimizing the recruitment of women for the "martyr death" as an adequate means for the rehabilitation of the family honor; if a woman has seriously harmed the moral notion and therefore disgraced her family; one way to atone the deed, is to commit a suicide attack, generally speaking, in order to regain her womanhood.[30]

Concluding:

"Terrorism is the intentional use of (or threat to use) violence aimed at civilians or against civilian targets in order to attain political aims", that is the definition of Terrorism according to Dr. Boaz Ganor's, who is the head of the ICT in Herzliya, Israel. Up until today there are approximately 110 different definitions for terrorism worldwide. Defining terrorism is one of the most important measures in order to counter terrorism on an international level. Terrorism has many fundamental aspects, such as psychological but also economic, political, religious and sociological.

Despite of the all in all strong involvement of women in Islamic terror organizations, one shouldn't and can't speak about a general appreciation of the women within the terrorist

---

[28] http://berlin.mfa.gov.il/mfm/web/main/document.asp?DocumentID=29265&MissionID=88
[29] http://www.anti-defamation.ch/index.php?id=5&section=2
[30] Middle East Media Research Institute (MEMRI) Internet Site, "Wafa Idris: The Celebration of the First Female Palestinian Suicide Bomber- Part I,II,III)", February, 2002 (www.memri.org)

organization. At the end of the day it is only a strategic decision of the individual terror organization, to which extent they implement women in their attacks.

Personal problems like being childless or unmarried are oftentimes motives of Islamic female suicide bombers; however it is also important to mention the main motive which is basically the occupation of Israel and its consequences.[31] Yet, there is no clear profile on a female suicide bomber, there is evidently a vast range of female attackers documented, from a 19 year old up to a grandmother.

There are no indications that women participate in the hierarchy of the organization and their relevant positions. Terrorist organizations implement female suicide terrorism in a systematic matter, which depends on the community. It is important to mention, that the patriarchal and conservative Palestinian society of the West Bank for instance, is more secular than the residents of the Gaza Strip, where today the Hamas and the Islamic Jihad are in power. In comparison to other Muslim societies, Palestinian women seem to have relatively more freedom and opportunities than Muslim women in Iraq, Iran, Saudi Arabia and other by male dominated Nations. Palestinian women are allowed to vote, hold office, drive cars and to own property. [32] Since they are relatively more involved in certain aspects of life, at the same time they become also active in suicide terrorism. From the moment female Palestinian suicide bombers kill Israelis; they are not anymore "just "women who died as martyrs, they rather reach "personal freedom", which they didn't get before.

In that respect, it would not only be cynical rather then simply wrong to speak of an emancipation of women within the Islamic society. Islamic Women are literally and symbolically "dying" to be more drawn into armed conflicts; nevertheless, it does not prevent them from being used by their society. When men carry out suicide operations, they most of the time are motivated by separatist or/and devoted extremism, a characteristic which is of course also collective regarding women. However, there still exists a difference between men and women suicide attackers, whereas women regard warfare as a means to break away from the predetermined life that is projected from them. When Islamic women become human weapons in the hands of men and terrorist organization, their objective is not necessarily to make a statement in the name of their country, religion, and leader; moreover they state a declaration in the name of their gender. It becomes one of the most extreme forms of

---

[31] http://www.kas.de/wf/de/33.12435/
[32] ICT Web Page: Clara Beyler "Messengers of Death-Female Suicide Bombers", February 2003 (www.ict.org.il/apage/10728.php) page.11

exploitation of women, who are being objectified even if they think that their choice is subjective.[33] The moment they decide and recognize their function, they automatically believe that their "choice" is subjective. Societies, especially western, tend to interpret their terroristic suicide actions as the product of an excessive and hopeless situation. The media again, plays an immense role, since the psychological effect of the audience legitimizes on one hand the actual act, such as the Islamic media, and on the other hand the western media condemns the act of terror by any means, above all regarding women within terrorist activities. This creates worldwide assumptions about the "weaker" sex, who are oppressed by the majority (men), not only because of religion or national origin, rather than because of their gender. The worldwide public opinion is being manipulated by terrorist organizations regarding the female participation in terrorism. As Donnely stated, "It is not a step forward in feminism but a step backward for humanity." [34]

In this moment the female suicide bomber acted like a man and had given up her female identity and above all her humanness. She became an almighty tyrant, which makes the female identity in this case uncertain. Female terrorist will always be defined by their gender within their terrorist organization and society; they become weapons in the hands of men and the terrorist organization rather than an essential part of the infrastructure. Orna Sasson-Levy once stated (2003): "Men *are* the military, women are *in* the military." In regard to this statement and the above discussed analysis, I came to the conclusion, that Islamic terrorism does have a gender, since female Islamic terrorists aim and stand "indirectly" for metaphoric and symbolism within a male dominated society. Islamic women take on traditional male roles in order to equalize within society. Gender roles within fundamental Islam are evidently set by men, which makes terrorism a male motivation and phenomenon within the female Islamic society.

---

[33] ICT Web Page: Clara Beyler "Messengers of Death-Female Suicide Bombers", February 2003 (www.ict.org.il/apage/10728.php) page 15
[34] ICT Web Page: Clara Beyler "Messengers of Death-Female Suicide Bombers", February 2003 (www.ict.org.il/apage/10728.php) page 13

References:

- ICT Web Page: Clara Beyler "Messengers of Death-Female Suicide Bombers", February 2003 (www.ict.org.il/apage/10728.php)
- Catharine Goldsmith, "Terrorists because They are Women" (Intersec, 1992) pp.26
- Elaine Donnelly, "The Suicide Sisterhood", National Review Online, April 26, 2002
- G.R. Perlstein and H.J. Vetter, "Woman and Terrorism: the Need for research", (Great Britain, 1991), pp. 96
- Islam On Line Internet Site, " Dareen Abu Aysheh: Number Two Woman Martyr" , www.islamonline.net/English/News/2002-02/28/article25.shtml
- Israel Embassy Internet Site, "The Exploitation of Palestinian Woman for Terrorism" (www.israelemb.org/articals/2002/April/2002042201.html)
- Middle East Media Research Institute (MEMRI) Internet Site, "Wafa Idris: The Celebration of the First Female Palestinian Suicide Bomber- Part I,II,III)", February, 2002 (www.memri.org)
- S. Jordan, "The Women Who Would Die for Allah," January 14, 2002. (www.newstatesman.com/print/200201140019)
- Waheeda Carvello, "The Impact of Marginalizing Women in the Islamic Movement", September, 2000 (www.muslimedia.com/archives/movement00/wom-move.htm)
- THE SOCIOLOGY AND PSYCHOLOGY OF TERRORISM: WHO BECOMES A TERRORIST AND WHY? A Report Prepared under an Interagency Agreement by the Federal Research Division, Library of Congress, September 1999, Author: Rex A. Hudson,Editor: Marilyn Majeska (www.fas.orf/irp/threat/frd.html)

- Speckhard, Anne. "Understanding Suicide Terrorism: Countering Human Bombs and Their Senders" in Topics in Terrorism: Toward a Transatlantic Consensus on the Nature of the Threat" (Volume I) Eds. Jason S. Purcell & Joshua D. Weintraub Atlantic Council Publication 2005
- Bloom, Mia. "Woman as Victims and Victimizers" (http://usinfo.state.gov/journals/itps/0507/ijpe/bloom.htm)
- Bloom, Mia "Female suicide bombers: A global trend", Daedalus Format, 2007
- Yoram Schweitzer ,Suicide Terrorism: Development & Characteristics, April 21, 2000 (http://www.ict.org.il/index.php?sid=119&lang=en&act=page&id=10729&str=yoram%20schweitzer)
- Rhiannon Talbot, "Myths in the representation of Women Terrorists" (Sage, 2000)
- Barbara Victor, *Army of Roses: Inside the World of Palestinian Women Suicide Bombers*. Rodale, 2003.
- http://plato.stanford.edu/entries/feminism-topics/
- http://www.datum.at/1005/stories/1113078
- http://lexicorient.com/e.o/assassins.htm